Triceratops
(try-SARE-ah-TOPS)

Spinosaurus
(SPY-no-saw-rus)

Kentrosaurus
(KEN-tro-saw-rus)

Tyrannosaurus rex
(ty-ran-oh-SAW-rus rex)

Dinosaurs, Dinosaurs by Byron Barton

Thomas Y. Crowell   New York

Dinosaurs, Dinosaurs Copyright © 1989 by Byron Barton Printed in the U.S.A. All rights reserved. 10 9 8 7 6 5 4 3 2 1 First Edition
Library of Congress Cataloging-in-Publication Data Barton, Byron. Dinosaurs, dinosaurs / Byron Barton.   p.   cm.
Summary: In prehistoric days there were many different kinds of dinosaurs, big and small, those with spikes and those with long sharp teeth.
ISBN 0-690-04768-1 (lib. bdg.) $ ISBN 0-694-00269-0 $ [1. Dinosaurs—Fiction.] I. Title. PZ7.B2848Di 1989
88-22938   (E)—dc19   CIP   AC

A long time ago

there were dinosaurs.

There were dinosaurs with horns

and dinosaurs with spikes.

There were dinosaurs with clubs

on their tails

and dinosaurs with armored plates.

There were

dinosaurs with sails on their backs

and dinosaurs with hard bony heads.

There were dinosaurs with long

sharp claws and long sharp teeth

and dinosaurs
with long, long necks
and long, long tails.

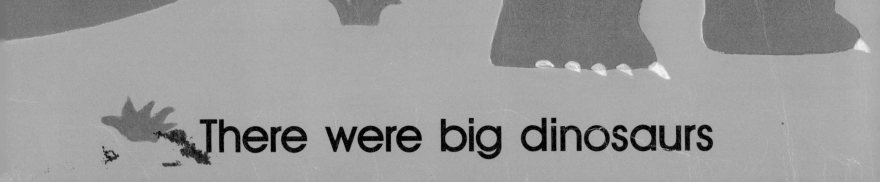

There were big dinosaurs

and small dinosaurs.

There were fierce dinosaurs

and scared dinosaurs.

There were hungry dinosaurs

and very tired and

very, very sleepy dinosaurs.

Dinosaurs, dinosaurs, a long time ago.

Stegosaurus
(steg-oh-SAW-rus)

Ankylosaurus
(an-KY-loh-SAW-rus)

Pachycephalosaurus
(PAK-ee-SEF-ah-loh-SAW-rus)

Diplodocus
(dip-LAH-doh-cuss)

Compsognathus
(komp-sog-NAY-thuss)

3

DATE DUE

OCT 31 1989	FEB 7 1990	OCT 4 1993	NO. 8 '05
NOV 8 1989	FEB 1 4 1991	DEC 1 6 1993	
DEC 1 2 1989	T-102	MAR 1 5	MAR 2010
JAN 5 1990	OCT 4 1991	T104	
FEB 1 5 1990	NOV 0 1991	OCT 2 '96	
FEB 2 8 1990	DEC 0 1991	T-103	
MAR 8 1990	DEC 1 7 1991	OCT 7 '97	
	OCT 6 1992	T 103	
APR 1 0 1990	OCT 2 8 1992	T-107	
APR 2 6 1990	FEB 2 4 1993	OCT 8 2002	
MAY 1 9 1990		DE 2	
OCT 1 8 1990	T 106	1 7 APR 2006	
NOV 27 1990	DEC 1 6 1992		
DEC 7 1990	T 115	2 6 APR 2006	
DEC 1 4 1990	T 117	1 1 OCT 2006	
JAN 0 8 1991	SEP 2 8 1993	2 OCT 2006	
JAN 2 4 1991	OCT 1 1993	2002 JUN 2	

HIGHSMITH 45-102   PRINTED IN U.S.A.